WRITERS
ON ...
LOVE

AMELIA CARRUTHERS

Copyright © 2014 Read Publishing Ltd

Edited by Amelia Carruthers
Designed by Zoë Horn Haywood

This book is copyright and may not be reproduced or copied in any way without the express permission of the publisher in writing.

British Library Cataloguing-in-Publication Data A catalogue record for this book is available from the British Library.

CONTENTS

Introduction   1

Defining Love   9

The Greeks and the Romans on Love   23

Religion on Love   35

The Renaissance on Love   45

The Long Nineteenth Century   59

The Twentieth Century   77

Love Letters   88

Romantics vs. Realists   97

Unrequited Love   111

Advice on Love   126

INTRODUCTION

What is love?

This simple question has troubled the greatest thinkers, from Plato to Petrarch and Shakespeare to Stendhal. There are many different theories that attempt to explain what love is, and what function it serves. However none seem to fully encompass the sheer complexity of feelings involved. It is at once highly subjective – unique to each individual, and at the same time a universal 'leveller' of human emotions. It would be very difficult to elucidate love to someone who had not experienced *love* or *being loved*. In fact to such a person 'love' would appear quite strange, if not overtly irrational. To those in love's deepest throws, it may appear just as unreasonable. Herein lies the dilemma.

The intricate and abstract nature of love often reduces discourse to a thought-terminating cliché, compressing the most far-reaching and multifaceted of human problems into concise, highly reductive, authoritative-sounding phrases. Statements such as Virgil's 'Love conquers all', or Thomas Aquinas defining love as 'to will the good of another' are prime examples. Bertrand Russell describes love as a condition of 'absolute value' (as opposed to relative value) whilst Gottfried Leibniz said that love is 'to be delighted by the happiness of another.' Compare these realistic and analytical statements with Oscar Wilde's love letter to Lord Alfred Douglas, noting the marvel 'that those red rose-leaf lips of yours should be made no less for the madness of music and song than for the madness of kissing', or Mark Twain's exhortation to Fanny Brawne that 'You have ravish'd me away by a Power I cannot resist: and yet I could resist till I saw you; and even since I have seen you I have endeavoured often "to reason against the reasons of my Love." I can do that no more.' All of the accounts above possess some kernel of truth, but the 'madness' of love shines through in the literary mind. As Francis Bacon noted, 'it is impossible to love, and to be wise.'

The word 'love' can have a variety of related but distinct meanings. Many other languages use multiple words to express the different concepts denoted under this one English term. The Ancient Greeks, for example, identified four forms of love: kinship or familiarity *(storge)*, friendship *(philia)*, sexual and/or romantic desire (eros) and self-emptying or divine love (agape). However with Greek (as with many other languages), it has been difficult to entirely separate the meanings of these words. In modern day usage, the term *s'agapo* means *I love you*, generally referring to the pure, ideal form of love, whereas the Greek word *erota* means *in love*. *Filo se* is yet another way to say *I love you,* whereas *Thelema* has come to mean *desire* in modern Greek.

The Christian understanding is that love comes from God. The love of man and woman (*eros* in Greek) and the unselfish love of others (*agape*), are often contrasted as 'ascending' and 'descending' love respectively, but are ultimately the same thing. Such beliefs have filtered into later Western European understandings of the term, with Andreas Capellanus's twelfth century treatise on 'Courtly Love' noting the fourth rule of love – that 'Love is always growing or diminishing.' Love may be patient, it may be kind, truthful, trusting and hopeful (Corinthians 13:4), but St. Peter's call to 'maintain constant love for one another' (Peter 4:8) is perhaps harder to follow than it first seems. In terms of this collection however, one important aspect to note is the *Romantic* concept of love, as differentiated from purely altruistic or erotic love.

Historians believe that the English word 'romance' developed from a vernacular dialect within the French language meaning 'verse narrative' – referring to the style of speech and writing of the elite classes. The word was originally a Latin adverb 'Romanicus', meaning *of the Roman Style.* The connecting notion is that medieval European tales were usually about chivalric adventure, not combining the idea of love until late into the seventeenth century. Such theories have been highly contested however, not least because of ancient evidence in the form of the 'worlds oldest love poem.' The Sumerian inscription, dating from the eighth century BCE was written on the occasion of a King's marriage:

Bridegroom, dear to my heart,
Goodly is your beauty, honeysweet,
Lion, dear to my heart,
Goodly is your beauty, honeysweet.

 The Roman poet Ovid also wrote a treatise on love, the *Ars Amatoria* (or, *The Art of Love*) which addresses, in depth, everything from extramarital affairs to overprotective parents. Despite this, many marriages or 'loving couples' were historically formed not for love itself, but more pragmatic reasons such as social, financial and political interests. It was only with the concept of *romantic love* however, that the idea of a 'narrative' was introduced to an individual's life. The rise of 'love' as we know it thus inextricably linked with the emergence of the medieval romance novel; linked to individualism, freedom and chivalry. Chevaliers (or knights) in the Middle Ages engaged in what were usually non-physical and non-marital relationships with the noble women whom they served. These associations were highly elaborate and steeped in a framework of tradition, which stemmed from theories of chivalric etiquette as a code of moral conduct.

Since marriage was commonly nothing more than a formal arrangement, this form of courtly love permitted expressions of emotional closeness (romance) which may have been lacking from traditional unions between husband and wife. Our present term 'courtship' also stems from this early tradition, spurring the connection between rendezvous, romances and love. As a result of such lines of thought, many satirists, writers and poets have highlighted (often cynically and entertainingly) how marriage and romance are not necessarily harmonious with each other. Shakespeare's *Romeo and Juliet,* Flaubert's *Madame Bovary* and Tolstoy's *Anna Karenina* all portray the 'tragic' contradiction between romance and societal constraints, with their protagonists driven to extreme acts in order to avoid matrimonial restrictions. Some like Ambrose Bierce, tackle the subject in a more jovial manner, simply defining love in *The Devil's Dictionary* as 'a temporary insanity curable by marriage.'

Consequently, a more sceptical literary tradition on the concept of love can be traced from Stendhal onwards. Stendhal's theory of crystallization implied 'an imaginative readiness for love', which only needed a single trigger for the object to be imbued with every fantasised perfection. Proust went further, stating that 'love is a striking example of how little reality means to us', singling out absence, inaccessibility or jealousy as the necessary precipitants of love. Nevertheless, 'love' as an emotion seems to fuel the creative impulse, driving writers to express both their most crushing lows and most exalted of joys. It is hard to imagine poetry and prose without it. With the ability to bring people of all genders, races, ages and social standing together, yet equally to drive them apart, love has provided centuries of inspiration to the world's best literary minds. As Alfred Lord Tennyson stated, ''Tis better to have loved and lost, than never to have loved at all.'

This collection is intended as a comprehensive introduction, across time and geographical location, to the world's most influential writers, and their thoughts on love. As the following excerpts and quotations will demonstrate, it is a sentiment as varied as it is universal, as primordial as it is contemporary; an irrational jumble of comedy, contradictions, and utmost understanding.

DEFINING LOVE

And now, said Socrates, I will ask about Love:— Is Love of something or of nothing?

Of something, surely, he replied.

Keep in mind what this is, and tell me what I want to know — whether Love desires that of which love is.

Yes, surely.

And does he possess, or does he not possess, that which he loves and desires?

Probably not, I should say.

Nay, replied Socrates, I would have you consider whether 'necessarily' is not rather the word. The inference that he who desires something is in want of something, and that he who desires nothing is in want of nothing, is in my judgment, Agathon, absolutely and necessarily true. What do you think?

I agree with you, said Agathon.

Very good. Would he who is great, desire to be great, or he who is strong, desire to be strong?

That would be inconsistent with our previous admissions.

True. For he who is anything cannot want to be that which he is?

Very true.

... Then now, said Socrates, let us recapitulate the argument. First, is not love of something, and of something too which is wanting to a man?

Yes, he replied.

Remember further what you said in your speech, or if you do not remember I will remind you: you said that the love of the beautiful set in order the empire of the gods, for that of deformed things there is no love — did you not say something of that kind?

Yes, said Agathon.

Yes, my friend, and the remark was a just one. And if this is true, Love is the love of beauty and not of deformity?

He assented.

And the admission has been already made that Love is of something which a man wants and has not?

True, he said.

Then Love wants and has not beauty?

Certainly, he replied.

And would you call that beautiful which wants and does not possess beauty?Certainly not.

Then would you still say that love is beautiful?

Agathon replied: I fear that I did not understand what I was saying.

You made a very good speech, Agathon, replied Socrates; but there is yet one small question which I would fain ask:— Is not the good also the beautiful?

Yes.

Then in wanting the beautiful, love wants also the good?

I cannot refute you, Socrates, said Agathon:— Let us assume that what you say is true.

Say rather, beloved Agathon, that you cannot refute the truth; for Socrates is easily refuted.

– Plato (*c*.428-348 BCE), *The Symposium* (*c*.385-380 BCE). *The Symposium* attempts to define the genesis, purpose and nature of 'love', and is now believed to be the origin of the concept of 'platonic love.' Socrates asserts that the highest purpose of love is to become a philosopher, or, literally, a *lover of wisdom*.

Love is composed of a single soul inhabiting two bodies.

– Aristotle (384-322 BCE), quoted in Diogenes Laërtius's *Lives of Eminent Philosophers*, thought to have been written in the first half of the third century CE.

For above all things, Love means sweetness, and truth, and measure; yea, loyalty to the loved one and to your word...

...And because of this I dare not meddle with so high a matter.

– Marie de France (twelfth century) – a French born medieval poet who lived in England and wrote at the court of King Henry II.

Love and the gentle heart are one thing,
as the wise man puts it in his verse,
and each without the other would be dust,
as a rational soul would be without its reason.
Nature, when she is loving, takes
Amor for lord, and the heart for his home,
in which sleeping he reposes
sometimes a short, sometimes a longer day.
Beauty may appear, in a wise lady,
so pleasant to the eyes, that in the heart,
is born a desire for pleasant things:
which stays so long a time in that place,
that it makes the spirit of Love wake.
And likewise in a lady works a worthy man.

– Dante Alighieri (*c.* 1265-1321) – *La Vita Nuova* (1295), 'Chapter XX – He is requested to say what love is.' Dante's *La Vita Nuova* details his love for Beatrice Portinari, who also served as the ultimate symbol of salvation in the *Divine Comedy*.

Love is a smoke made with the fume of sighs;

Being purged, a fire sparkling in lovers' eyes;

Being vexed, a sea nourished with loving tears.

What is it else? A madness most discreet,

A choking gall, and a preserving sweet.

– William Shakespeare (1564-1616), Romeo speaking to Benvolio in Act I, scene 1, of *Romeo and Juliet* (*c.* 1591).

LOVE IS A CANVAS FURNISHED BY NATURE AND EMBROIDERED BY IMAGINATION.

– François-Marie Arouet, better known by his nom de plume: Voltaire (1694-1778).

There are four different kinds of love:

1. Passionate Love. This was the love of the Portuguese nun, that of Heloïce for Abelard, of the captain of Vésel, and of the gendarme of Cento.

2. Mannered Love. Which flourished in Paris about 1760... A stylized painting, this, where the rosy hues extend into the shadows, where there is no place for anything at all unpleasant – for that would be a breach of etiquette, of good taste, of delicacy, and so forth...

3. Physical Love. You are hunting; you come across a handsome young peasant girl who takes to her heels through the woods. Everyone knows the love that springs from this kind of pleasure, and however desiccated and miserable you may be, this is where your Love-life begins at sixteen.

4. Vanity-Love. The great majority of men, especially in France, both desire and possess a fashionable woman, much in the way one might own a fine horse – as a luxury befitting a young man. Vanity, a little flattered and a little piqued, leads to enthusiasm. Sometimes there is physical love, but not always; often even physical pleasure is lacking...

The happiest version of this insipid relationship is where physical pleasure grows with habit. Then memories produce a semblance of love; there is the pricking at your pride and the sadness in satisfaction; the atmosphere of romantic fiction catches you by the throat, and you believe yourself lovesick and melancholy, for vanity will always pretend to be grand passion. One thing is certain though: whichever kind of love produces the pleasures, they only become vivid, and their recollection compelling, from the moment of inspiration. In love, unlike most other passions, the recollection of what you have had and lost is always better than what you can hope for in the future.

– Marie-Henri Beyle, better known as 'Stendhal' (1783-1842). In this extract from *On Love* (1822), Stendhal attempts to rationally analyse this most obscure of human emotions by scientifically outlining the four 'main types' of love.

While [the Poetic Principle] itself is, strictly and simply, the Human Aspiration for Supernal Beauty, the manifestation of the Principle is always found in *an elevating excitement of the Soul* — quite independent of that passion which is the intoxication of the Heart — or of that Truth which is the satisfaction of the Reason. For, in regard to Passion, alas! its tendency is to degrade, rather than to elevate the Soul. Love, on the contrary — Love ... is unquestionably the purest and truest of all poetical themes. And in regard to Truth — if, to be sure, through the attainment of a truth, we are led to perceive a harmony where none was apparent before, we experience, at once, the true poetical effect — but this effect is preferable to the harmony alone, and not in the least degree to the truth which merely served to render the harmony manifest.

– Edgar Allen Poe (1809-1849), providing a compelling riposte to the problems of definition for both *poetry* and *love,* in his essay 'The Poetic Principle'. It was published posthumously in 1850

If science does not produce love it is insufficient... Moral love places the centre of the individual in the centre of being. It has at least salvation in principle, the germ of eternal life. To love is virtually to know; to know is not virtually to love; there you have the relation of these two modes of man. The redemption wrought by science or by intellectual love is then inferior to the redemption wrought by will or by moral love. The first may free a man from himself, it may enfranchise him from egotism. The second drives the ego out of itself, makes it active and fruitful. The one is critical, purifying, negative; the other is vivifying, fertilizing, positive... Therefore do not amend by reasoning, but by example; approach feeling by feeling; do not hope to excite love except by love. Be what you wish others to become. Let yourself and not your words preach for you.

– Henri Amiel (1821-1881), a Swiss theorist, poet and critic. Underappreciated with contemporaries, *Amiel's Journal* (published in 1882) is now considered a masterpiece of philosophy. In this passage, from 7th April 1851, Amiel (in a similar way to Poe) provides a definition for the hitherto diametrically opposed concepts of *Science* and *Love*.

Perhaps the feelings that we experience when we are in love represent a normal state. Being in love shows a person who he should be.

– Anton Pavlovich Chekhov (1860-1904) – one of the greatest short story writers in history. Chekhov also practiced as a medical doctor throughout most of his literary career, stating that 'Medicine is my lawful wife... and literature is my mistress.'

Love, n. A temporary insanity curable by marriage.

– Ambrose Bierce (1842-1914), *The Devil's Dictionary* (1911). Bierce was an American editorialist, journalist and short story writer, most famed for his satirical lexicon, *The Devil's Dictionary*. His motto 'nothing matters' alongside his sardonic view of human nature and the wider world earned him the nickname 'Bitter Bierce'

LOVE IS SPACE AND TIME

MEASURED BY HEART.

– Marcel Proust (1871-1922), the author of *À La Recherche du Temps Perdu* ('In Search of Lost Time'), considered by many to be one of the greatest authors of all time.

THE GREEKS AND THE ROMANS ON LOVE

Love is all we have, the only way that each can help the other.

– *Euripides* (*c.*480-406 BCE), *Orestes* (408 BCE); a play which follows the events of Orestes after he murders his mother. Euripides was one of the three great tragedians of classical Athens, alongside Aeschylus and Sophocles.

Oh, if I had Orpheus' voice and poetry
with which to move the Dark Maid and her Lord,
I'd call you back, dear love, from the world below.
I'd go down there for you. Charon or the grim
King's dog could not prevent me then
from carrying you up into the fields of light.

> – *Euripides, Alcestis* (438 BCE). The oldest surviving work of Euripides, *Alcestis* is an ambiguous, tragicomic play, conversely described as 'cheerfully romantic' or 'bitterly ironic.' Here, Admetus is mourning the death of his beloved wife.

At the touch of love, everyone becomes a poet.

The madness of love is the greatest of heaven's blessings...

> – Plato (*c.*428-348 BCE), from *The Symposium* and the *Phaedrus* (c.370 BCE) respectively. The latter text is ostensibly about the topic of pure love, but also revolves around rhetoric (the art of discourse) and erotic love.

For pleasure is a state of soul, and to each man that which he is said to be a lover of is pleasant.... Now for most men their pleasures are in conflict with one another because these are not by nature pleasant, but the lovers of what is noble find pleasant the things that are by nature pleasant; and virtuous actions are such... Happiness then is the best, noblest, and most pleasant thing in the world, and these attributes are not severed as in the inscription at Delos: Most noble is that which is justest, and best is health; but pleasantest is it to win what we love.

(*Nicomachean Ethics,* Book I, 1099.a6)

The young have exalted notions, because they have not been humbled by life or learned its necessary limitations.... All their mistakes are in the direction of doing things excessively and vehemently. They overdo everything; they love too much, hate too much, and the same with everything else.

(*Rhetoric,* Book II, 1389.a31)

– Aristotle (384-322 BCE). The *Nicomachean Ethics* and the *Rhetoric* are Aristotle's most detailed discussions of the issue of love. Like Plato, Aristotle equates it with intrinsic goodness. 'Love' (*or friendship*) is defined as 'wishing for someone the things that he deems good, for the sake of that person and not oneself, and the accomplishment of these things to the best of one's ability.'

The Passion of Love

This craving 'tis that's Venus unto us:
From this, engender all the lures of love,
From this, O first hath into human hearts
Trickled that drop of joyance which ere long
Is by chill care succeeded. Since, indeed,
Though she thou lovest now be far away,
Yet idol-images of her are near
And the sweet name is floating in thy ear.
But it behooves to flee those images;
And scare afar whatever feeds thy love;
And turn elsewhere thy mind; and vent the sperm,
Within thee gathered, into sundry bodies,
Nor, with thy thoughts still busied with one love,
Keep it for one delight, and so store up
Care for thyself and pain inevitable.

– Lucretius (99-55 BCE) was a Roman poet and philosopher. His only known work is the epic philosophical poem, *De Rerum Natura,* quoted above ('Book IV'). Dealing with the tenets of Epicureanism the manuscript depicts a universe guided by physical principles and chance. In this view, 'pleasure' is the greatest good, but the way to attain such pleasure is to live modestly and to limit one's desires.

Love is the attempt to form a friendship inspired by beauty.

– Marcus Tullius Cicero (106-43 BCE), the Roman philosopher, politician and orator, quoted by Michel de Montainge (1533-1592), the pioneering French essayist. In the essay 'Of Friendship' (1580) Montaigne continues, 'If you press me to tell why I love him, I feel that this cannot be expressed, except by answering: Because it was he, because it was I.'

LOVE CONQUERS ALL; AND WE MUST YIELD TO LOVE.

– Virgil (70-19 BCE), *Eclogues,* 'Book X' (37 BC). In this famous pronouncement, we see the culmination of Virgil's first major work – and the transformation of a remote, mountainous region of Greece (the text's setting) into the original and ideal place of pastoral song.

If you want to be loved, be lovable.

Ars Amatoria ('The Art of Love')

Love yields to business. If you seek a way out of love, be busy; you'll be safe then.

Remedia Amoris ('The Cure for Love')

– Ovid (43 BCE – 17 CE). Although best known for his *Metamorphoses*, Ovid also gave relationship advice. *Remedia Amoris* was written as a companion to the *Ars Amoria* – offering strategies to avoid being hurt by love, or how to fall out of love. The *Ars Amatoria* was written to show a man how to court a woman, and how subsequently to keep her. Ovid later wrote a third book, advising women how to keep the love of men, saying 'I have just armed the Greeks against the Amazons; now, Penthesilea, it remains for me to arm thee against the Greeks.'

Love in its essence is spiritual fire.

– Lucius Annaeus Seneca (*c.* 4 – 65 CE). Seneca (the younger) was a Roman philosopher, statesman and dramatist who was forced to commit suicide for alleged complicity in a plot to assassinate the Emperor Nero.

You will not believe what a longing for you possesses me. The chief cause of this is my love; and then we have not grown used to be apart. So it comes to pass that I lie awake a great part of the night, thinking of you; and that by day, when the hours return at which I was wont to visit you, my feet take me, as it is so truly said, to your chamber, but not finding you there I return, sick and sad at heart, like an excluded lover. The only time that is free from these torments is when I am being worn out at the bar, and in the suits of my friends. Judge you what must be my life when I find my repose in toil, my solace in wretchedness and anxiety. Farewell.

– Pliny the Younger (61-113 CE), writing to his third wife, Calpurnia (date unknown).

... You know that many censure boy-loves for their instability, and jeeringly say that that intimacy like an egg is destroyed by a hair, for that boy-lovers like Nomads, spending the summer in a blooming and flowery country, at once decamp then as from an enemy's territory... But this charge cannot justly be brought against genuine lovers, and it was prettily said by Euripides, as he embraced and kissed handsome Agatho whose beard was just sprouting, that the Autumn of beautiful youths was lovely as well as the Spring. And I maintain that the love of beautiful and chaste wives flourishes not only in old age amid grey hairs and wrinkles, but even in the grave and monument. And while there are few such long unions in the case of boy-loves, one might enumerate ten thousand such instances of the love of women, who have kept their fidelity to the end of their lives.

– Plutarch (46-120 CE), *On Love* (date unknown). Pederasty was a firmly established Greek tradition of erotic relationships between adult males (the erastes) and younger males (the eromenos), the latter usually in their early teens. Debates over the relative merits of homosexual and heterosexual love were commonplace in this period, with equally strong views on either side. Plutarch himself was an advocate of heterosexual married love.

But tell me this: did you never love any person, a young girl, or slave, or free? What then is this with respect to being a slave or free? Were you never commanded by the person beloved to do something which you did not wish to do? Have you never flattered your little slave? Have you never kissed her feet? And yet if any man compelled you to kiss Caesar's feet, you would think it an insult and excessive tyranny. What else, then, is slavery? Did you never go out by night to some place whither you did not wish to go, did you not expend what you did not wish to expend, did you not utter words with sighs and groans, did you not submit to abuse and to be excluded?

– Epictetus (55-135 CE), a Greek sage and Stoic philosopher – speaking of love's darker side. Whilst love itself was not seen as bad, it was important for the Stoics that it did not degenerate into an 'involved arrangement', where healthy enjoyment quickly led to harmful infatuation.

Sexual love is a desire which does not afflict virtuous men.

– Diogenes Laërtius (third Century CE), *Lives of Eminent Philosophers.* According to Laërtius, the Stoics held that 'wise men should have their wives in common, so that anyone might make love to any woman.' The Stoics taught that destructive emotions (i.e. romantic jealousy) resulted from errors in judgment, and that a 'sage', or person of 'moral and intellectual perfection', would not suffer such emotions.

RELIGION ON LOVE

Being deeply loved by someone gives you strength, while loving someone deeply gives you courage.

Love is of all passions the strongest, for it attacks simultaneously the head, the heart and the senses.

– Lao-Tzu (usually dated to around the sixth century BCE), was a philosopher and a poet of ancient China, best known as the reputed author of the *Tao Te Ching* and the founder of philosophical Taoism. Lao-Tzu is also revered as a deity in religious Taoism and many traditional Chinese religions, which emphasise living in harmony with the *Tao* (meaning 'path' or 'principle' – something that is both the source and driving force behind everything that exists).

Do not seek perfection in a changing world. Instead, perfect your love.

Love in the past is only a memory. Love in the future is a fantasy. Only here and now can we truly love.

In the end these things matter most: How well did you love? How fully did you live? How deeply did you learn to let go?

– *The Teachings of Buddha* – passed down over many centuries as oral tradition. According to Buddhist tradition, the Buddha lived and taught in the eastern part of the Indian subcontinent sometime between the sixth and fourth centuries BCE. 'Love' forms one of the brahmaviharas, or the 'four immeasurables' alongside compassion, joy and equanimity.

Love the Lord your God with all your heart and with all your soul and with all your mind and with all your strength. The second is this: 'Love your neighbour as yourself.' There is no commandment greater than these.

– The Bible, Mark, 12:31. Within these two commandments lies the basis of the Christian faith.

Love is patient, love is kind. It does not envy, it does not boast, it is not proud. It is not rude, it is not self-seeking, it is not easily angered, it keeps no record of wrongs. Love does not delight in evil but rejoices with the truth. It always protects, always trusts, always hopes, always perseveres. Love never fails. But where there are prophecies, they will cease; where there are tongues, they will be stilled; where there is knowledge, it will pass away.

– The Bible, Corinthians, 13:4. The most popular passage for readings at Church of England wedding ceremonies.

Daughters of Jerusalem, I charge you: Do not arouse or awaken love until it so desires. Who is this coming up from the desert leaning on her lover? Under the apple tree I roused you; there your mother conceived you, there she who was in labor gave you birth. Place me like a seal over your heart, like a seal on your arm; for love is as strong as death, its jealousy unyielding as the grave. It burns like blazing fire, like a mighty flame. Many waters cannot quench love; rivers cannot wash it away. If one were to give all the wealth of his house for love, it would be utterly scorned.

– *The Bible*, Song of Solomon, 8:4.

And among His signs is that He has created for you, of yourselves, mates that you may feel tranquillity and relief in them; and He has set love and mercy between you. There are signs in this for a people who reflect.

– *The Quran*, 30:21. Whilst love, even within marriage was condemned by many early societies, this verse proclaims the spiritual and emotional attachment between people as a cause for celebration and reflection.

Those who believe and do good deeds – the Gracious God will create love in their hearts.

– *The Quran*, 19:97.

When a man loves his brother, he should tell him that he loves him.

– Abu Dawud (817 CE -889 CE), a noted Persian collector who compiled the third of the six 'canonical' hadith collections recognised by Sunni Muslims, the *Sunan Abi Dawid*. Love in the form of friendship is an important part of the Islamic faith.

LOVE IS THE BEAUTY OF THE SOUL.

– Saint Augustine (354-430), an early Christian theologian and philosopher, who 'established anew the ancient faith.'

Lord, grant that I might not so much seek to be loved as to love.

– Francis of Assisi (1181/82-1226). Frances of Assisi was an Italian Catholic friar and preacher, known as the patron saint of animals and the environment.

Accustom yourself continually to make many acts of love, for they enkindle and melt the soul.

– Saint Teresa of Ávila (1515-1582), a prominent Spanish mystic, Roman Catholic saint, Carmelite nun, and integral part of the Counter Reformation.

Faith makes all things possible... love makes all things easy.

– Dwight L. Moody (1837-1899); an American evangelist and publisher who founded the Moody Church in Chicago, Illinois.

Out of the Indian approach to life
there comes a great freedom –
an intense and absorbing love for nature;
a respect for life;
enriching faith in a Supreme Power;
and principles of truth, honesty, generosity, equity,
and brotherhood as a guide to mundane relations.

> – Luther Standing Bear (1868-1939), an Oglala Lakota chief who fought to preserve Lakota heritage and tradition. Standing Bear's commentaries on Native American wisdom educated the American public, and highlighted their holistic, loving and respectful approach to nature.

Love is the only reality and it is not a mere sentiment. It is the ultimate truth that lies at the heart of creation.

> – Rabindranath Tagore (1861-1941), Tagore is considered one of the greatest writers in modern Indian literature – a Bengali poet, novelist and teacher who won the Nobel Prize for Literature in 1913.

A coward is incapable of exhibiting love; it is the prerogative of the brave.

– Mahatma Gandhi (1869-1948); the pre-eminent leader of Indian nationalism in British ruled India, who inspired movements for civil rights and freedom across the world. Ghandi's vision was for a free India based on religious pluralism, and his non-violent civil disobedience was largely inspired by the Hindu teachings of love and equality.

THE RENAISSANCE ON LOVE

And when she finds one who is worthy to behold her, he feels her power, for what she bestows on him is restorative, and humbles him, so that he forgets any injury. Moreover God has made the power of her grace even greater, for no one who has spoken with her can come to a bad end.

– Dante Alighieri (1265-1321), *Vita Nuova* (1295). Here, the pursuit of a lover is not considered a sin, but a virtue. Dante portrays the lady's beauty as the fullest example of nature's ability to reveal God's love. The character was inspired by Beatrice Portinari, whom he first met when he was only nine.

Love is the crowning grace of humanity, the holiest right of the soul, the golden link which binds us to duty and truth, the redeeming principle that chiefly reconciles the heart to life, and is prophetic of eternal good.

– Francesco Petrarca, commonly anglicized as Petrarch (1304-1374), as quoted in *Notable Thoughts about Women: A Literary Mosaic* (1882). Petrarch was an Italian scholar and poet of the Renaissance, and one of the earliest humanists.

Upon this a question arises: whether it be better to be loved than feared or feared than loved? It may be answered that one should wish to be both, but, because it is difficult to unite them in one person, is much safer to be feared than loved, when, of the two, either must be dispensed with. Because this is to be asserted in general of men, that they are ungrateful, fickle, false, cowardly, covetous, and as long as you succeed they are yours entirely; they will offer you their blood, property, life and children, as is said above, when the need is far distant; but when it approaches they turn against you... Men have less scruple in offending one who is beloved than one who is feared, for love is preserved by the link of obligation which, owing to the baseness of men, is broken at every opportunity for their advantage.

– Niccolò Machiavelli (1469-1527), *The Prince*, 'Chapter XVII' (published 1532). In this chapter, possibly the most well-known of the text, Machiavelli offers a purely pragmatic justification to the question of whether it is better to be loved or feared. Fear provides a means to an end (security for the prince), whereas love does not.

Love is when he gives you a piece of your soul, that you never knew was missing.

– Torquato Tasso (1594-1595), an Italian poet best known for his work 'Jerusalem Delivered' (1580). Tasso suffered from mental illness and died a few days before he was due to be crowned as the 'King of Poets' by the Pope.

Love looks not with the eyes but with the mind.
And therefore is winged Cupid painted blind.

– William Shakespeare (1564-1616), *Midsummer Night's Dream,* Act I, scene 1.

Let Rome in Tiber melt, and the wide arch
Of the rang'd empire fall! Here is my space.
Kingdoms are clay; our dungy earth alike
Feeds beast as man. The nobleness of life
Is to do thus [embracing], when such a mutual pair
And such a twain can do't, in which I bind,
On pain of punishment, the world to weet
We stand up peerless.

– William Shakespeare, *Antony and Cleopatra,* Act I, scene 1 (1606) – Antony proclaiming his all-consuming love for Cleopatra.

Let me not to the marriage of true minds
Admit impediments. Love is not love
Which alters when it alteration finds,
Or bends with the remover to remove:
O, no! it is an ever-fixed mark,
That looks on tempests and is never shaken;
It is the star to every wandering bark,
Whose worth's unknown, although his height be taken.
Love's not Time's fool, though rosy lips and cheeks
Within his bending sickle's compass come;
Love alters not with his brief hours and weeks,
But bears it out even to the edge of doom.
    If this be error and upon me proved,
    I never writ, nor no man ever loved.

– William Shakespeare, (1564-1616), 'Sonnet 116' (published in 1609).

Wrong not, sweet empress of my heart,
The merit of true passion,
With thinking that he feels no smart,
That sues for no compassion;

Since, if my plaints serve not to approve
The conquest of thy beauty,
It comes not from defect of love,
But from excess of duty.

For, knowing that I sue to serve
A saint of such perfection,
As all desire, but none deserve,
A place in her affection,

I rather choose to want relief
Than venture the revealing;
Where glory recommends the grief,
Despair distrusts the healing.

Thus those desires that aim too high
For any mortal lover,
When reason cannot make them die,
Discretion doth them cover.

Yet, when discretion doth bereave
The plaints that they should utter,
Then thy discretion may perceive
That silence is a suitor.

Silence in love bewrays more woe
Than words, though ne'er so witty:
A beggar that is dumb, you know,
May challenge double pity.

Then wrong not, dearest to my heart,
My true, though secret, passion:
He smarteth most that hides his smart,
And sues for no compassion.

– Walter Raleigh (1552-1618), 'The Silent Lover' (date unknown). Raleigh was an English aristocrat, writer, poet, soldier, spy, explorer – and court favourite of Queen Elizabeth I.

It is a strange thing, to note the excess of this passion, and how it braves the nature, and value of things, by this; that the speaking in a perpetual hyperbole, is comely in nothing but in love. Neither is it merely in the phrase; for whereas it hath been well said, that the arch-flatterer, with whom all the petty flatterers have intelligence, is a man's self; certainly the lover is more. For there was never proud man thought so absurdly well of himself, as the lover doth of the person loved; and therefore it was well said, That it is impossible to love, and to be wise.... By how much the more, men ought to beware of this passion, which loseth not only other things, but itself!

– Sir Francis Bacon (1561-1626), 'Chapter X, Of Love', from *The Works of Francis Bacon* (published 1765).

Twice or thrice had I lov'd thee,
Before I knew thy face or name;
So in a voice, so in a shapeless flame
Angels affect us oft, and worshipp'd be;
Still when, to where thou wert, I came,
Some lovely glorious nothing I did see.
But since my soul, whose child love is,
Takes limbs of flesh, and else could nothing do,
More subtle than the parent is
Love must not be, but take a body too;
And therefore what thou wert, and who,
I bid Love ask, and now
That it assume thy body, I allow,
And fix itself in thy lip, eye, and brow.

Whilst thus to ballast love I thought,
And so more steadily to have gone,
With wares which would sink admiration,
I saw I had love's pinnace overfraught;
Ev'ry thy hair for love to work upon
Is much too much, some fitter must be sought;
For, nor in nothing, nor in things
Extreme, and scatt'ring bright, can love inhere;
Then, as an angel, face, and wings
Of air, not pure as it, yet pure, doth wear,
So thy love may be my love's sphere;
Just such disparity
As is 'twixt air and angels' purity,
'Twixt women's love, and men's, will ever be.

– John Donne (1572-1631), 'Air and Angels.' Donne was a celebrated English poet and a cleric in the Church of England. Here resurrecting the legitimacy of sensuous, bodily love.

It lies not in our power to love or hate,
For will in us is overruled by fate.
When two are stripped, long ere the course begin,
We wish that one should love, the other win;

And one especially do we affect
Of two gold ingots, like in each respect:
The reason no man knows; let it suffice
What we behold is censured by our eyes.
Where both deliberate, the love is slight:
Who ever loved, that loved not at first sight?

– Christopher Marlowe (1564-1593), from 'Hero and Leander' (published 1598). After Marlowe's untimely death, the poem was completed by George Chapman.

My dearest dust, could not thy hasty day
Afford thy drowsy patience leave to stay
One hour longer: so that we might either
Sit up, or gone to bed together?
But since thy finished labour hath possessed
Thy weary limbs with early rest,
Enjoy it sweetly; and thy widow bride
Shall soon repose her by thy slumbering side;
Whose business, now, is only to prepare
My nightly dress, and call to prayer:
Mine eyes wax heavy and the day grows old,
The dew falls thick, my blood grows cold.
Draw, draw the closed curtains: and make room:
My dear, my dearest dust; I come, I come.

– Lady Catherine Dyer (1641). The inscription above appears on an alabaster and black marble monument, to the left of the altar in Colmworth Church (Bedfordshire, England).
  It is dedicated to Sir William Dyer, and was erected by his widowed wife, Catherine.

Absence sharpens love, presence strengthens it.

– Thomas Fuller (1608-1661). Fuller was a prolific author, best known for his *Worthies of England,* and was one of the first English writers able to live by his pen (and his many patrons).

WHEN LOVE IS NOT MADNESS, IT IS NOT LOVE.

– Pedro Calderón de la Barca (1600-1681), a dramatist, poet and writer of the Spanish Golden Age – honouring the time honoured tradition of linking true love with true insanity.

Love ceases to be a pleasure when it ceases to be a secret.

– Aphra Behn (1640-1689), *The Lover's Watch,* 'Four o'Clock General Conversation' (1686). A prolific dramatist of the English Restoration, Behn was one of the first English professional female writers. Along with Delarivier Manley and Eliza Haywood, she is referred to as part of 'The fair triumvirate of wit.'

Follow love and it will flee, flee love and it will follow thee.

– John Gay (1685-1732), an English poet and dramatist, best known for his satirical *The Beggar's Opera* (1728).

THE LONG NINETEENTH CENTURY

O my Luve's like a red, red rose
That's newly sprung in June;
O my Luve's like the melodie
That's sweetly play'd in tune.

As fair art thou, my bonnie lass,
So deep in luve am I:
And I will luve thee still, my dear,
Till a' the seas gang dry:

Till a' the seas gang dry, my dear,
And the rocks melt wi' the sun:
I will luve thee still, my dear,
While the sands o' life shall run.

And fare thee well, my only Luve
And fare thee well, a while!
And I will come again, my Luve,
Tho' it were ten thousand mile.

– Robert Burns (1759-1796), Scotland's national poet; 'A Red Red Rose' (1794). This poem formed part of Burns's attempt to preserve traditional Scottish folk songs.

Love seeketh not Itself to please,
Nor for itself hath any care;
But for another gives its ease,
And builds a Heaven in Hell's despair.

So sung a little Clod of Clay,
Trodden with the cattle's feet;
But a Pebble of the brook,
Warbled out these metres meet:

Love seeketh only self to please,
To bind another to Its delight,
Joys in another's loss of ease,
And builds a Hell in Heaven's despite.

– William Blake (1757-1827), *The Clod and the Pebble,* published as part of his collection *Songs of Experience* (1794).

We are all born for love. It is the
principle of existence, and its only end.

– Isaac D'Israeli (1766-1848), a British writer, scholar and man of letters, best known
for his essays and correspondence – and as the father of British Prime Minister
Benjamin Disraeli.

Love and Friendship Opposed

A person once said to me, that he could make nothing of love, except that it was friendship accidentally combined with desire. Whence I concluded that he had never been in love. For what shall we say of the feeling which a man of sensibility has towards his wife with her baby at her breast! How pure from sensual desire! Yet how different from friendship!

Sympathy constitutes friendship; but in love there is a sort of antipathy, or opposing passion. Each strives to be the other, and both together make up one whole.

– Samuel Taylor Coleridge (1772-1834), *Specimens of the Table Talk* – extract from 27th September 1830. Coleridge was an English poet, critic and philosopher, who, alongside his friend William Wordsworth, was a founder of the Romantic Movement.

What is so pleasant as these jets of affection which make a young world for me again? What is so delicious as a just and firm encounter of two, in a thought, in a feeling? How beautiful, on their approach to this beating heart, the steps and forms of the gifted and the true!

– Ralph Waldo Emerson (1803-1882), 'Essay VI – Friendship' (1841). A transcendentalist nature writer, Emerson believed that God, or the divine, suffuses life, and that reality can be understood by fully immersing oneself in the natural world.

When one has once fully entered the realm of love, the world — no matter how imperfect — becomes rich and beautiful, it consists solely of opportunities for love.

– Søren Kierkegaard (1813 – 1855) in *Works of Love* (1847), a text which deals primarily with the Christian conception of agape love, in contrast with erotic love (eros) or preferential love (phileo).

He's more myself than I am. Whatever our souls are made of, his and mine are the same.

– Emily Bronte (1818-1848), *Wuthering Heights* (1847), Catherine speaking of her love for Heathcliff.

It was many and many a year ago,
   In a kingdom by the sea,
That a maiden there lived whom you may know
   By the name of Annabel Lee;
And this maiden she lived with no other thought
   Than to love and be loved by me.
I was a child and *she* was a child,
   In this kingdom by the sea,
But we loved with a love that was more than love—
   I and my Annabel Lee—
With a love that the wingèd seraphs of Heaven
   Coveted her and me...

– Edgar Allen Poe (1809-1849), 'Annabel Lee' (1849) – the last complete poem composed by Poe. Like so many of his works, it explores the theme of the death of a beautiful woman.

A LOVING HEART IS THE TRUEST WISDOM.

– Charles Dickens (1812-1870), *David Copperfield*, 'Chapter IX' (1850).

Nevertheless the flames did die down – whether exhausted from lack of supplies or choked by excessive feeding. Little by little, love was quenched by absence; regret was smothered by routine; and the fiery glow that had reddened her pale sky grew grey and gradually vanished... But the storm kept raging, her passion burned itself to ashes, no help was forthcoming, no new sun rose to the horizon. Night closed in completely around her, and she was left alone in a horrible void of piercing cold.

– Gustave Flaubert (1821-1880), *Madame Bovary* (1856), 'Part II, Chapter VII' – the story of a doctor's wife, Emma Bovary, who has adulterous affairs and lives well beyond her means in order to escape the banalities and emptiness of provincial life.

Blow again trumpeter! and for thy theme,
Take now the enclosing theme of all, the solvent and the setting,
Love, that is pulse of all, the sustenance and the pang,
The heart of man and woman all for love,
No other theme but love — knitting, enclosing, all-diffusing love.

– Walt Whitman (1819-1892), 'The Mystic Trumpeter' from *Leaves of Grass* (1855). As a nature writer, Whitman was part of the transition between transcendentalism of Thoreau, Emerson and Muir, and the realism of later American writers such as William Dean Howells and Stephen Crane. Today, he is celebrated as one of the most influential poets in the American canon and the father of 'free verse.'

Love is knowing that even when you are alone, you will never be lonely again. The supreme happiness of life is the conviction that we are loved – loved for ourselves, or rather, loved in spite of ourselves; this conviction the blind have.... Are they deprived of anything? No. Light is not lost where love enters.

– Victor Hugo (1802-1885), *Les Misérables* (1862).

I like not only to be loved, but also to be told I am loved. I am not sure that you are of the same kind. But the realm of silence is large enough beyond the grave. This is the world of light and speech, and I shall take leave to tell you that you are very dear.

– Mary Ann Evans (1819-1880), better known by her pen name, George Eliot, writing in 1875 to Georgiana Burne-Jones, the wife of the artist Edward Burne-Jones.

What is hell? I maintain that it is the suffering of being unable to love.

– Fyodor Dostoyevsky (1821-1881) – *The Brothers Karamazov* (1880); Dostoyevsky's last philosophical and spiritual masterpiece.

Love is anterior to life,
Posterior to death,
Initial of creation, and
The exponent of breath.

– Emily Dickinson (1830-1886), 'XXXVII' from *Complete Poems* (published 1924). Whilst Dickinson was a prolific private poet, few of her poems were published during her lifetime.

Love a friend, love a wife, something, whatever you like, but one must love with a lofty and serious intimate sympathy, with strength, with intelligence, and one must always try to know deeper, better, and more.

– Vincent Van Gogh (1853-1890), writing to his brother in July of 1880 – exactly ten months before he shot himself in the chest.

Its difficult to know at what moment love begins; it is less difficult to know that it has begun.

– Henry Wadsworth Longfellow (1807-1882), an American poet and educator, best known for *The Song of Hiawatha* and *Evangeline*. He was also the first American to translate Dante's *Divine Comedy*.

Women wish to be loved without a why or a wherefore; not because they are pretty, or good, or well bred, or graceful, or intelligent, but because they are themselves. All analysis seems to them to imply a loss of consideration, a subordination of their personality to something which dominates and measures it. They will have none of it; and their instinct is just. As soon as we can give a reason for a feeling we are no longer under the spell of it; we appreciate, we weigh, we are free, at least in principle. Love must always remain a fascination, a witchery, if the empire of woman is to endure. Once the mystery gone, the power goes with it. Love must always seem to us indivisible, insoluble, superior to all analysis, if it is to preserve that appearance of infinity, of something supernatural and miraculous, which makes its chief beauty. The majority of beings despise what they understand, and bow only before the inexplicable. The feminine triumph par excellence is to convict of obscurity that virile intelligence which makes so much pretence to enlightenment. And when a woman inspires love, it is then especially that she enjoys this proud triumph. I admit that her exultation has its grounds. Still, it seems to me that love — true and profound love — should be a source of light and calm, a religion and a revelation, in which there is no place left for the lower victories of vanity. Great souls care only for what is great, and to the spirit which hovers in the sight of the Infinite, any sort of artifice seems a disgraceful puerility.

– Henri Amiel (1821-1881), *Amiel's Journal,* 17th March 1868, considering women's experience of love.

A flower cannot blossom without sunshine, and man cannot live without love.

– Max Müller (1823-1900), a German-born philologist and Orientalist.

Songs of longing!

And they will resound in my letters, just as they always have, sometimes loudly and sometimes secretly so that you alone can hear them... But they will also be different — different from how they used to be, these songs. For I have turned and found longing at my side, and I have looked into her eyes, and now she leads me with a steady hand.

– Rainer Maria Rilke (1875-1926) writing to his lover, Lou Andreas-Solomé on 3rd June 1897. Despite near constant rejections from the married Solomé, Rilke persevered and the two went on to have a thirty-five year long relationship.

THE TWENTIETH CENTURY

A pair of lovers are like sunset and sunrise: there are such things every day but we very seldom see them.

- Samuel Butler (1835-1902), a British novelist and satirist; 'Chapter XI' from *The Way of All Flesh* (published in 1903).

Love is the only way to rescue humanity from all ills, and in it you too have the only method of saving your people from enslavement... Love, and forcible resistance to evil-doers, involve such a mutual contradiction as to destroy utterly the whole sense and meaning of the conception of love...

– An extract from Tolstoy's long letter to the Indian revolutionary, Taraknath Das, who asked for Tolstoy's support in their struggle for independence. It was written on 14th December 1908, and was read by Mahatma Ghandi, who asked Tolstoy's permission to publish it in the newspaper, *Indian Opinion*. The exchange sparked a life-long correspondence between Ghandi and Tolstoy.

I am just crazy about Margaret Armstrong and I have the most awful crush on her that ever was. This has been the case ever since Bob's party. She is not pretty but I think she is very attractive looking. She is extremely graceful and a very good dancer and the most interesting talker I have ever seen or rather heard....

Jim Portfield and I were invited to call on Elizabeth Dean by Elizabeth and when we got there we found *her* too and we started out for a walk. Margaret and Jim walked ahead and Elizabeth and I behind. This made me mad and this was further inflamed when they got a block ahead of us. Then Elizabeth told me some things. She said that Margaret had given her a note the day before in school which said 'I know I am fickle but I like Jim just as much as I do Scott.' When I learned this I was jealous of Jim as I had never been of anyone before. I said some ridiculous things about how I was going to get even with him in Margaret's estimation when we reached the country club. Elizabeth went ahead and asked Margaret which of us she liked the best. Margaret said she liked me best. All the way home I was in the seventh heaven of delight.

– A teenage F. Scott Fitzgerald (1896-1940), writing in his diary on 24th February 1910.

The Bible tells us to love our neighbours, and also to love our enemies; probably because they are generally the same people.

– G. K. Chesterton (1874-1936), writing in the *Illustrated London News* (16th July 1910).

Between the finite and the infinite

The missing link of Love has left a void.

Supply the link, and earth with Heaven will join

In one continued chain of endless life.

– Ella Wheeler Wilcox (1850-1919), an American author and poet; 'The Way' in *New Thought Pastels* (1913).

You don't want to love – your eternal and abnormal craving is to be loved. You aren't positive, you're negative. You absorb, absorb, as if you must fill yourself up with love, because you've got a shortage somewhere.

– D.H. Lawrence (1885-1930), *Sons and Lovers* (1913). While the novel initially incited a lukewarm critical reception, along with allegations of obscenity, it is today regarded as a masterpiece and as Lawrence's finest achievement.

Love has no age, no limit, and no death.

– John Galsworthy (1867-1933), *'Indian Summer of a Forsyte'* (1918), part of the three-part *The Forsyte Saga* – a text which chronicles the life and loves of a large upper-middle class English family.

At any rate, let us love for a while, for a year or so, you and me. That's a form of divine drunkenness that we can all try. There are only diamonds in the whole world, diamonds and perhaps the shabby gift of disillusion.

– An adult F. Scott Fitzgerald, in 'The Diamond As Big as the Ritz', *Tales of the Jazz Age*, (1922).

Love has no other desire but to fulfil itself.
But if you love and must needs have desires, let these be your desires:
To melt and be like a running brook that sings its melody to the night.
To know the pain of too much tenderness.
To be wounded by your own understanding of love;
And to bleed willingly and joyfully.
To wake at dawn with a winged heart and give thanks for another day of loving;
To rest at the noon hour and meditate love's ecstasy; to return home at eventide with gratitude;
And then to sleep with a prayer for the beloved in your heart and a song of praise upon your lips.

– Khalil Gibran (1883-1931), a Lebanese artist, poet and writer, chiefly known for his 1923 part-fictional, part-philosophical work, *The Prophet*.

It is sad not to love, but it is much sadder not to be able to love.

– Miguel de Unamuno (1864-1936), a Spanish essayist, novelist and playwright. From 'To a Young Writer' (date unknown).

Life has taught us that love does not consist of gazing at each other, but in looking outward in the same direction.

– Antoine de Saint Exupéry (1900-1944), a French aristocrat, writer, poet and pioneering aviator – in *Terre des Hommes* (translated into English as *Wind, Sand and Stars*), published in 1939.

At the height of being in love the boundary between ego and object threatens to melt away. Against all the evidence of his senses, a man who is in love declares that 'I' and 'you' are one, and is prepared to behave as if it were a fact.

– Sigmund Freud (1856-1939), *Civilization and its Discontents* (1929) – outlining the inevitable clashes between the individual's quest for freedom and civilisation's demand for conformity. Freud argues that whilst the love instinct (eros) can be commandeered by society to bind its members together, there is also an aggressive instinct which must be either repressed or directed against a rival culture.

LOVE LETTERS

Venice, 18th October 1503.

...I shall never rest content until I am certain she knows what she is able to enact in me and how great and strong is the fire that her great worth has kindled in my breast. The flame of true love is a mighty force, and most of all when two equally matched wills in two exalted minds contend to see which loves the most, each striving to give yet more vital proof...

May your Ladyship beseech her to perform whatever you feel is best for me. With my heart I kiss your Ladyship's hand, since I cannot with my lips.

– Pietro Bembo (1470-1547), an Italian scholar, literary theorist and cardinal. Bembo was also one of the most respected poets of his day. This letter was written to Lucrezie Borgia who was the daughter of the Spanish cardinal, Rodrigo Borgia, later Pope Alexander VI.

To my Mistress.

Because the time seems very long since I heard concerning your health and you, the great affection I have for you has induced me to send you this bearer, to be better informed of your health and pleasure, and because, since my parting from you, I have been told that the opinion in which I left you is totally changed, and that you would not come to court either with your mother, if you could, or in any other manner; which report, if true, I cannot sufficiently marvel at, because I am sure that I have since never done any thing to offend you, and it seems a very poor return for the great love which I bear you to keep me at a distance both from the speech and the person of the woman that I esteem most in the world: and if you love me with as much affection as I hope you do, I am sure that the distance of our two persons would be a little irksome to you, though this does not belong so much to the mistress as to the servant.

Consider well, my mistress, that absence from you grieves me sorely, hoping that it is not your will that it should be so; but if I knew for certain that you voluntarily desired it, I could do no other than mourn my ill-fortune, and by degrees abate my great folly. And so, for lack of time, I make an end of this rude letter, beseeching you to give credence to this bearer in all that he will tell you from me.

Written by the hand of your entire Servant,
H.R.

– Henry VIII to Anne Boleyn (written in July 1527); from a collection of letters held in the Vatican Library. Henry's affair with Anne Boleyn led to the schism with the Catholic church and the start of the English reformation – when Pope Charles V refused to grant an annulment to Henry's marriage with Catherine of Aragon.

I am a prisoner here in the name of the King; they can take my life, but not the love that I feel for you. Yes, my adorable mistress, to-night I shall see you, and if I had to put my head on the block to do it.

For heaven's sake, do not speak to me in such disastrous terms as you write; you must live and be cautious; beware of madame your mother as of your worst enemy. What do I say? Beware of everybody; trust no one; keep yourself in readiness, as soon as the moon is visible; I shall leave the hotel incognito, take a carriage or a chaise, we shall drive like the wind to Sheveningen; I shall take paper and ink with me; we shall write our letters.

If you love me, reassure yourself; and call all your strength and presence of mind to your aid; do not let your mother notice anything, try to have your pictures, and be assured that the menace of the greatest tortures will not prevent me to serve you. No, nothing has the power to part me from you; our love is based upon virtue, and will last as long as our lives. Adieu, there is nothing that I will not brave for your sake; you deserve much more than that. Adieu, my dear heart!

Arout
(Voltaire)

– Voltaire to Catherine Olympre Dunoyer, sent from The Hague in 1713. Whilst serving as secretary to the French ambassador in the Netherlands, Volaitre fell in love with a young French protestant refugee; Catherine. Their scandalous elopement was foiled by Voltaire's father however, and the young man was forced to return to France. Voltaire had many troubles with the authorities for his critiques of the government and religious intolerance. These activities were to result in numerous imprisonments and exiles over his lifetime.

21st November 1796

I am going to bed with my heart full of your adorable image... I cannot wait to give you proofs of my ardent love... How happy I would be if I could assist you at your undressing, the little firm white breast, the adorable face, the hair tied up in a scarf a la creole. You know that I will never forget the little visits, you know, the little black forest... I kiss it a thousand times and wait impatiently for the moment I will be in it. To live within Joséphine is to live in the Elysian fields. Kisses on your mouth, your eyes, your breast, everywhere, everywhere.

November 1796

I don't love you anymore; on the contrary, I detest you. You are a vile, mean, beastly slut. You don't write to me at all; you don't love your husband; you know how happy your letters make him, and you don't write him six lines of nonsense...
Soon, I hope, I will be holding you in my arms; then I will cover you with a million hot kisses, burning like the equator.

– Napoleon Bonaparte to Joséphine de Beauharnais, written during his campaigns in Italy of 1797. Her beauty was infamous, and after their meeting in 1795, Bonaparte was infatuated. They married in 1796 (despite social disapproval, as Joséphine was a widowed mother of two), but in the same year she began an affair with a handsome Hussar lieutenant Hippolyte Charles – rumours of which infuriated Bonaparte. Six days after writing the first letter, he returned to her apartment in Milan, to find it empty. Suspecting she was with Charles, Napoleon's love turned to jealousy.

My angel, my all, my own self — only a few words today, and that too with pencil (with yours) — only till tomorrow is my lodging definitely fixed. What abominable waste of time in such things — why this deep grief, where necessity speaks?

Can our love persist otherwise than through sacrifices, than by not demanding everything? Canst thou change it, that thou are not entirely mine, I not entirely thine? Oh, God, look into beautiful Nature and compose your mind to the inevitable. Love demands everything and is quite right, so it is for me with you, for you with me — only you forget so easily, that I must live for you and for me — were we quite united, you would notice this painful feeling as little as I should...

...We shall probably soon meet, even today I cannot communicate my remarks to you, which during these days I made about my life — were our hearts close together, I should probably not make any such remarks. My bosom is full, to tell you much — there are moments when I find that speech is nothing at all. Brighten up — remain my true and only treasure, my all, as I to you. The rest the gods must send, what must be for us and shall.

Your faithful
Ludwig

– From Ludwig van Beethoven (1770-1827) to an unidentified 'Immortal Beloved', written on 6th July, 1812.

Dearest Fanny,

My sweet love, I shall wait patiently till tomorrow before I see you, and in the mean time, if there is any need of such a thing, assure you by your Beauty, that whenever I have at any time written on a certain unpleasant subject, it has been with your welfare impress'd upon my mind. How hurt I should have been had you ever acceded to what is, notwithstanding, very reasonable! How much the more do I love you from the general result! In my present state of Health I feel too much separated from you and could almost speak to you in the words of Lorenzo's Ghost to Isabella:
'Your Beauty grows upon me and I feel
A greater love through all my essence steal.'
My greatest torment since I have known you has been the fear of you being a little inclined to the Cressid; but that suspicion I dismiss utterly and remain happy in the surety of your Love, which I assure you is as much a wonder to me as a delight. Send me the words 'Good night' to put under my pillow.

Your affectionate
J.K.

– John Keats to Fanny Brawne, written in February 1820. Keats was completely in love with Fanny, to the point is caused him great anxiety and ill health. When Tuberculosis took hold and he was advised by his doctors to move to a warmer climate, Keats left for Italy in September 1820, knowing he would never see Brawne again. He died five months later, after which Brawne stayed in mourning for six years.

My dearest Teresa,

I have read this book in your garden;–my love, you were absent, or else I could not have read it. It is a favourite book of yours, and the writer was a friend of mine. You will not understand these English words, and others will not understand them,–which is the reason I have not scrawled them in Italian. But you will recognize the handwriting of him who passionately loved you, and you will divine that, over a book which was yours, he could only think of love.

In that word, beautiful in all languages, but most so in yours–*Amor mio*–is comprised my existence here and hereafter. I feel I exist here, and I feel I shall exist hereafter,–to what purpose you will decide; my destiny rests with you, and you are a woman, eighteen years of age, and two out of a convent. I love you, and you love me,–at least, you say so, and act as if you did so, which last is a great consolation in all events.

But I more than love you, and cannot cease to love you. Think of me, sometimes, when the Alps and ocean divide us, –but they never will, unless you wish it.

– Lord Byron to Countess Teresa Guiccioli, written in August 1819. Teresa was just nineteen when she met the thirty-one year old Byron, but their ensuing love affair was legendary. When Byron was struck down with a fever, the Countess stayed by his bedside until she was physically removed by her husband and banned from seeing him again. Byron had many romances and scandals, one other particularly notable affair with the also married Lady Caroline Lamb – who gave him the now famous epitaph of 'mad, bad and dangerous to know.'

My beloved angel,

I am nearly mad about you, as much as one can be mad: I cannot bring together two ideas that you do not interpose yourself between them. I can no longer think of nothing but you. In spite of myself, my imagination carries me to you. I grasp you, I kiss you, I caress you, a thousand of the most amorous caresses take possession of me. As for my heart, there you will always be — very much so. I have a delicious sense of you there. But my God, what is to become of me, if you have deprived me of my reason? This is a monomania which, this morning, terrifies me. I rise up every moment say to myself, 'Come, I am going there!' Then I sit down again, moved by the sense of my obligations. There is a frightful conflict. This is not a life. I have never before been like that. You have devoured everything. I feel foolish and happy as soon as I let myself think of you. I whirl round in a delicious dream in which in one instant I live a thousand years. What a horrible situation! Overcome with love, feeling love in every pore, living only for love, and seeing oneself consumed by griefs, and caught in a thousand spiders' threads. O, my darling Eva, you did not know it. I picked up your card. It is there before me, and I talked to you as if you were here. I see you, as I did yesterday, beautiful, astonishingly beautiful. Yesterday, during the whole evening, I said to myself 'She is mine!' Ah! The angels are not as happy in Paradise as I was yesterday!

– Honoré de Balzac to Ewelina Ha'n'ska in June 1835. The two had a passionate affair, and intensely corresponded. Ha'n'ska promised to marry Balzac on the death of her husband, but her family prevented this pairing by threatening to contest Ha'n'ska's inheritance. Fearful she and her daughter would be left destitute, Ha'n'ska wrote to Balzac in 1841 stating simply 'You are free.' The couple eventually married in March of 1850, but Balzac died just four months after the wedding, leaving Ha'n'ska distraught.

My Own Boy,

Your sonnet is quite lovely, and it is a marvel that those red rose-leaf lips of yours should be made no less for the madness of music and song than for the madness of kissing. Your slim gilt soul walks between passion and poetry. I know Hyacinthus, whom Apollo loved so madly, was you in Greek days.

Why are you alone in London, and when do you go to Salisbury? Do go there to cool your hands in the grey twilight of Gothic things, and come here whenever you like. It is a lovely place and lacks only you; but go to Salisbury first.

Always, with undying love, yours,
Oscar

– Oscar Wilde to Lord Alfred 'Bosie' Douglas. Wilde met Douglas in June of 1891 and the young man became Wilde's muse, confidant and lover. Wilde, who was earning up to £100 a week from his plays, indulged Douglas's every whim: material, artistic or sexual. By 1893 Wilde was infatuated with Douglas and they consorted together regularly in a tempestuous affair – which eventually led to Wilde's trial for 'gross indecency with other men', subsequent conviction to two year's hard labour, and final self-exile to France.

ROMANTICS VS. REALISTS

By all means, marry. If you get a good wife, you'll become happy; if you get a bad one, you'll become a philosopher.

– Socrates (b. unknown – d. 399 BCE); the founder of Western philosophy and husband to Xanthippe.

Bringing love and wine together is adding fuel to the fire ... If you really want to know what she [or he] is like, look at her by daylight, and when you're sober.

– Ovid (43 BCE – C.18 CE), relationship advice from *Ars Amatoria*, 'The Art of Love', written in 2 CE.

And herof men saye a comyn proverbe in England that love lasteth as longe as the money endureth and whan the money faylleth than there is no love.

– William Caxton (1420-1492), the first English printer and publisher – as well as an author in his own right. This matter-of-fact observation comes from *The Game and Playe of the Chesse*, 'Book III' (1474).

LOVE AND EGGS ARE BEST WHEN THEY ARE FRESH.

– Old Russian Proverb.

Things simply good can never be unfit;
She's fair as any, if all be like her;
And if none be, then she is singular.
All love is wonder; if we justly do
Account her wonderful, why not lovely too?
Love built on beauty, soon as beauty, dies;
Choose this face, changed by no deformities.
Women are all like angels; the fair be
Like those which fell to worse; but such as she,
Like to good angels, nothing can impair:
'Tis less grief to be foul, than to have been fair.

– John Donne (1572-1631), 'Elegy II: The Anagram', published in *The Poems of John Donne* (1896).

HE THAT FALLS IN LOVE WITH HIMSELF WILL HAVE NO RIVALS.

– Benjamin Franklin (1706-1790), one of the Founding Father's of the United States –
proving the prudence of self-love.

Love is my religion – I could die for that – I could die for you.

– John Keats (1795-1821), writing to Fanny Brawne (his neighbour and lover) on 13th October 1819. Keats was one of the main figures of the second generation of Romantic poets, along with Lord Byron and Percy Bysshe Shelley.

Romantic love is an illusion. Most of us discover this truth at the end of a love affair or else when the sweet emotions of love lead us into marriage and then turn down their flames.

– Thomas Moore (1779-1852), an Irish poet, singer and songwriter. Moore was responsible, alongside John Murray, for burning Lord Byron's memoirs after his death.

Love is not altogether a delirium... yet it has many points in common therewith.... As in common Madness, it is Fantasy that superadds itself to sight.

– Thomas Carlyle (1795-1881), a Scottish philosopher, satirical writer, essayist and historian of the Victorian era. From *Sartor Resartus* (meaning 'The tailor re-tailored), published in 1836.

Marry

Children — (if it Please God) — Constant companion, (& friend in old age) who will feel interested in one, — object to be beloved & played with. — better than a dog anyhow.— Home, & someone to take care of house — Charms of music & female chit-chat. — These things good for one's health. — but terrible loss of time. —

My God, it is intolerable to think of spending one's whole life, like a neuter bee, working, working, & nothing after all. — No, no won't do. — Imagine living all one's day solitarily in smoky dirty London House. — Only picture to yourself a nice soft wife on a sofa with good fire, & books & music perhaps — Compare this vision with the dingy reality of Grt. Marlbro' St.

Not Marry

Freedom to go where one liked — choice of Society & little of it. — Conversation of clever men at clubs — Not forced to visit relatives, & to bend in every trifle. — to have the expense & anxiety of children — perhaps quarelling — Loss of time. — cannot read in the Evenings — fatness & idleness — Anxiety & responsibility — less money for books &c — if many children forced to gain one's bread. — (But then it is very bad for ones health[19] to work too much)

Perhaps my wife wont like London; then the sentence is banishment & degradation into indolent, idle fool —

— Charles Darwin (1809-1882), diary entry from 7th April 1838 — in true scientific manner, debating the pros and cons of marriage. He decided it was 'proved necessary to marry' and then went on to debate the relative merits of marrying 'soon or late.'

I hold it true, whate'er befall;
I feel it when I sorrow most;
'Tis better to have loved and lost
Than never to have loved at all.

– Alfred Lord Tennyson (1809-1892), from 'In Memoriam A.H.H.' (1849); a requiem for the poet's beloved Cambridge friend Arthur Henry Hallam, who died suddenly of a cerebral haemorrhage. The poem was written over the course of seventeen years.

A pair of powerful spectacles has sometimes sufficed to cure a person in love.

– Friedrich Nietzche (1844-1900), the German philosopher famed for the concept of 'life affirmation', which embraces the realities of the world in which we live over the idea of a world beyond.

When one is in love, one always begins by deceiving one's self, and one always ends by deceiving others. That is what the world calls a romance.

– Oscar Wilde (1854-1900). 'Chapter Four', from *The Picture of Dorian Gray* (1890) – Lord Henry speaking to Dorian.

I ask not, 'Is thy hope still sure,
Thy love still warm, thy faith secure?'
I ask not, 'Dream'st thou still of me? –
Longest alway to fly to me?' –
    Ah, no – but as the sum includeth all
        The good gifts of the Giver,
    I sum all these in asking thee,
        'O sweetheart, how's your liver?'

But Indigestion hath the power
To mar the soul's serenest hour –
To crumble adamantine trust,
And turn its certainties to dust –
To dim the eye with nameless grief –
To chill the heart with unbelief –
To banish hope, & faith, & love,
Place heaven below & hell above.

For if thy liver worketh right,
Thy faith stands sure, thy hope is bright,
Thy dreams are sweet, and I their god,
Doubt threats in vain—thou scorn'st his rod.
    Keep only thy digestion clear,
    No other foe my love doth fear.

Then list – details are naught to me
    So thou'st the *sum*-gift of the Giver –
I ask thee all in asking thee,
    'O darling, how's your liver?'

– Samuel Langhorne Clemens, better known as Mark Twain (1835-1910), 'Love Song' written at a German health resort in 1891-1982. This comical, tongue-in-cheek ode to 'true love' was first published in St. Louis's *Medical Fortnightly* on 15th *May 1892.*

Love came at dawn, when all the world was fair,
When crimson glories' bloom and sun were rife;
Love came at dawn, when hope's wings fanned the air,
    And murmured, 'I am life.'

Love came at eve, and when the day was done,
When heart and brain were tired, and slumber pressed;
Love came at eve, shut out the sinking sun,
    And whispered, 'I am rest.'

– Mark Twain, 'Love Came at Dawn' (1896), this time a truly sincere and touching meditation on the nature of love. The poem is a tribute to his daughter, Susy who died of Meningitis in August of 1896 – at the age of twenty-four. After this loss, Twain was left heartbroken and fell into a deep depression.

We don't believe in rheumatism and true love until after the first attack.

– Marie von Ebner-Eschenbach (1830-1916), an Austrian writer regarded as one of the most important German-language authors of the nineteenth century.

Love is a striking example of how little reality means to us.

– Marcel Proust (1871-1922), from *À La Recherche du Temps Perdu*, his monumental novel published in seven parts between 1913 and 1927.

UNREQUITED LOVE

One is never too old to yearn.

– Old Italian Proverb

I hate the day, because it lendeth light
To see all things, but not my love to see.

– Edmund Spenser (1552-1599), one of the greatest poets of Modern English verse,
'Daphnaïda, An Elegy' (1591), on the death of Lady Douglas Howard.

A mighty pain to love it is,
And 'tis a pain that pain to miss;
But of all pains, the greatest pain
It is to love, but love in vain.

– Abraham Cowley (1618-1667), one of the leading English poets of the seventeenth century. 'Gold' published in 1656, is a musing on the ability of money to monopolise love, which ends with the regrettable refrain that *'Gold,* alas, does *Love beget.'*

If we must part forever,
Give me but one kind word to think upon,
And please myself with, while my heart's breaking.

– Thomas Otway (1652-1685), *The Orphan, or The Unhappy Marriage* (Act III, scene 1), written in 1680. Otway was an English dramatist of the Restoration period, famed for his tragic masterpieces in the style of Shakespeare.

Must it ever be thus-that the source of our happiness must also be the fountain of our misery? The full and ardent sentiment which animated my heart with the love of nature, overwhelming me with a torrent of delight, and which brought all paradise before me, has now become an insupportable torment, a demon which perpetually pursues and harasses me.

– Johann Wolfgang von Goethe (1749-1832), *The Sorrows of Young Werther* (1774).
Werther is speaking of his insatiable love for Lotte – who is already engaged to another man.

THE PLEASURE OF LOVE LASTS ONLY A MOMENT

THE GRIEF OF LOVE LASTS A LIFETIME...

– Jean Pierre Claris De Florian (1755-1794), a French poet and romance writer. 'Plaisir d'amour' (meaning *The Pleasure of Love*) – which was turned into a classical French love song, and set to music by Jean-Paul-Égide Martini (1784).

O stay, sweet warbling woodlark stay,
Nor quit for me the trembling spray,
A hapless lover courts thy lay,
Thy soothing, fond complaining.
Again, again that tender part,
That I may catch thy melting art;
For surely that wad touch her heart
Wha kills me wi' disdaining.
Say, was thy little mate unkind,
And heard thee as the careless wind?
Oh, nocht but love and sorrow join'd,
Sic notes o' woe could wauken!
Thou tells o' never-ending care;
O'speechless grief, and dark despair:
For pity's sake, sweet bird, nae mair!
Or my poor heart is broken!

– Robert Burns (1759-1796), 'Address to the Woodlark', a poem sent in a letter to his friend George Thomson in April 1795.

Love is never lost. If not reciprocated, it will flow back and soften and purify the heart.

– Washington Irving (1783-1859), an American essayist, biographer and diplomat, best known for his short stories *Rip Van Winkle* (1819) and *The Legend of Sleepy Hollow* (1820).

I watched thee when the foe was at our side,
Ready to strike at him – or thee and me,
Were safety hopeless – rather than divide
Aught with one loved save love and liberty.

I watched thee on the breakers, when the rock,
Received our prow, and all was storm and fear,
And bade thee cling to me through every shock;
This arm would be thy bark, or breast thy bier.

I watched thee when the fever glazed thine eyes,
Yielding my couch and stretched me on the ground
When overworn with watching, ne'er to rise
From thence if thou an early grave hadst found.

The earthquake came, and rocked the quivering wall,
And men and nature reeled as if with wine.
Whom did I seek around the tottering hall?
For thee. Whose safety first provide for? Thine.

And when convulsive throes denied my breath
The faintest utterance to my fading thought,
To thee – to thee – e'en in the gasp of death
My spirit turned, oh! oftener than it ought.

Thus much and more; and yet thou lov'st me not,
And never wilt! Love dwells not in our will.
Nor can I blame thee, though it be my lot
To strongly, wrongly, vainly love thee still.

– Lord Byron (1788-1824), one of the greatest English Romantic poets, who had many passionate love affairs. 'Love and Death' was one of the last poems Byron wrote before he died (published 1887). It was addressed to Lukas Chalandritsanos, a fifteen year old Greek boy, Byron's page – who did not return his affections.

Quasimodo then lifted his eye to look upon the gypsy girl, whose body, suspended from the gibbet, he beheld quivering afar, under its white robes, in the last struggles of death; then again he dropped it upon the archdeacon, stretched a shapeless mass at the foot of the tower, and he said with a sob that heaved his deep breast to the bottom, 'Oh-all that I've ever loved!'

– Quasimodo, the deformed bell ringer and protagonist of Victor Hugo's *The Hunch Back of Notre Dame* (1831), holding the body of Esmeralda – the one citizen who showed any kindness to him. On her death, Quasimodo murdered the priest who betrayed her, and then lay with her corpse until he died of starvation.

Only three things are infinite: the sky in its stars, the sea in its drops of water, and the heart in its tears.

– Gustave Flaubert (1821-1880), writing to Louise Colet on 9th August, 1846. His affair with Colet was Flaubert's only serious romantic relationship, although he never married.

As the gambler said of his dice, to love and win is the best thing. To love and lose, the next best.

– William M. Thackeray (1811-1863), *The History of Pendennis* (1848-1850). Thackeray was an English novelist famed for his satirical works, particularly *Vanity Fair* (1848), a panoramic portrait of English society.

The unqualified truth is, that when I loved Estella with the love of a man, I loved her simply because I found her irresistible. Once for all; I knew to my sorrow, often and often, if not always, that I loved her against reason, against promise, against peace, against hope, against happiness, against all discouragement that could be. Once for all; I loved her nonetheless because I knew it, and it had no more influence in restraining me, than if I had devoutly believed her to be human perfection.

– Charles Dickens (1812-1870), Pip speaking of Estella in *Great Expectations* (1861). Pip is fascinated by Estella and spends many years in her company, even though he has been warned she has been brought up to inspire unrequited love in the men around her.

Yet leave me not; yet, if thou wilt, be free;
Love me no more, but love my love of thee.
Love where thou wilt, and live thy life; and I,
One thing I can, and one love cannot – die.

– Algernon Charles Swinburne (1837-1909), an English poet, playwright and novelist. The stanza comes from his poem 'Erotion' (1865).

Love, unrequited, robs me of my rest:
Love, hopeless love, my ardent soul encumbers:
Love, nightmare-like, lies heavy on my chest,
And weaves itself into my midnight slumbers!

– Sir William S. Gilbert (1836-1911), an English dramatist, poet and illustrator. The quotation forms the first stanza of his comical poem, 'The Lord Chancellor's Song' (date unknown).

Let no one who loves be called altogether unhappy, even love unreturned has its rainbow.

– J. M. Barrie (1860-1937), best known as the creator of *Peter Pan*. The quotation comes from *The Little Minister* (1891) – a sentimental novel following a young impoverished minister in a Scottish weaving village.

There is something beautiful, touching and poetic when one person loves more than the other, and the other is indifferent.

– Anton Chekov (1860-1904), 'After the Theatre' – a short story capturing the morbid, romantic imagination of a sixteen year-old theatre goer. It was published in *The Bet, and Other Stories* in 1915.

It was all love on my side, and all good comradeship and friendship on hers. When we parted she was a free woman, but I could never again be a free man.

– Sir Arthur Conan Doyle (1859-1930), 'The Adventure of the Abbey Grange' (1904); one of fifty-six *Sherlock Holmes* short stories – and one of the thirteen to be collected in *The Return of Sherlock Holmes*.

We are never so defenceless against suffering as when we love, never so helplessly unhappy as when we have lost our loved object or its love.

– Sigmund Freud (1856-1939), *Civilization and its Discontents* (1929).

He would not stay for me, and who can wonder?
  He would not stay for me to stand and gaze.
I shook his hand, and tore my heart in sunder,
  And went with half my life about my ways.

– A.E. Housman (1859-1936), an English classical scholar and poet, best known for his cycle of lyrical poems, *A Shropshire Lad*. This short verse is taken from Housman's *Additional Poem's* (published in 1939).

ADVICE ON LOVE

Love is like warfare... The night, winter, long marches, cruel suffering, painful toil, all these things have to be borne by those who fight in Love's campaigns ... If the ordinary, safe route to your mistress is denied you, if her door is shut against you, climb up on to the roof and let yourself down by the chimney, or the skylight. How it will please her to know the risks you've run for her sake! 'Twill be an earnest of your love.'

– More relationship advice from Ovid's *Ars Amatoria* (2 CE).

Accept the things to which fate binds you and love the people with whom fate brings you together, but do so with all your heart.

– Marcus Aurelius (121-180 CE), Roman Emperor from 161-180 CE, and the last of the 'Five Good Emperors.' Marcus Aurelius is also considered one of the most important Stoic philosophers.

His first words shall test her mind and probe her wish in a manner so ambiguous as to leave her a way of certain escape by making it possible for her to pretend not to see that his talk is actually of love.

– Baldassare Castiglione (1478-1529), an Italian courtier, diplomat and author. *The Book of the Courtier* (1528), providing advice on how to approach, for the first time, a woman you love...

Why so pale and wan, fond lover?
Prithee, why so pale?
Will, when looking well can't move her,
Looking ill prevail?
Prithee, why so pale?

Why so dull and mute, young sinner?
Prithee, why so mute?
Will, when speaking well can't win her,
Saying nothing do 't?
Prithee, why so mute?

Quit, quit, for shame; this will not move,
This cannot take her.
If of herself she will not love,
Nothing can make her.
The devil take her!

– Sir John Suckling (1609-1641), an English poet renowned for his careless gaiety and wit,
'Song' (1638) – offering some friendly advice over the 'one that got away.'

Brute force or bribes of diamonds

Bend others to your will,

But gentle words have greater power

And gain more conquests still.

– Charles Perrault (1628-1703), the author of *Cinderella, Sleeping Beauty* and *Puss in Boots*, on the power of 'gentle words'; the 'Second Moral' from *Perrault's Fairy Tales*, first published as *Tales of Mother Goose* in 1697.

Keep your eyes wide open before marriage, half shut afterwards.

– Benjamin Franklin (1706-1790) – a polymath, author, politician and 'The First American.'

THE MORE ONE JUDGES,
THE LESS ONE LOVES.

– Honoré de Balzac (1799-1850), in *Physiologie Du Mariage* (1829); a treatise on marriage that Balzac wrote whilst still a single man.

Don't walk in front of me, I may not follow. Don't walk behind me, I may not lead. There is only one happiness in life, to love and be loved.

– George Sand (1804-1876), who threw off the bonds of a loveless marriage in 1831, in order to search for a 'great romance.'

There is no remedy for love but to love more.

– Henry David Thoreau (1817-1862), an American naturalist and transcendentalist. From a journal entry on 25th July 1839, five days after meeting Ellen Sewall for the first time. Thoreau's brother John also loved Sewall, but she rejected both brother's proposals.

Life is short and we have never too much time for gladdening the hearts of those who are travelling the dark journey with us. Oh, be swift to love, make haste to be kind!

– Henri Frédéric Amiel (1821-1881), a Swiss philosopher, poet and critic, who lost both his parents at an early age.

You can give without loving, but you can never love without giving. The great acts of love are done by those who are habitually performing small acts of kindness.

– Victor Hugo (1802-1885), *Les Misérables* (1862).

It is true that, in poetizing love, we assume in those we love qualities that are lacking in them, and that is a source of continual mistakes and continual miseries for us. But to my thinking it is better, even so; that is, it is better to suffer than to find complacency on the basis of woman being woman and man being man.

– Anton Chekov (1860-1904), *Ariadne* (1895), on the importance of combating simple contentment.

Keep love in your heart. A life without it is like a sunless garden when the flowers are dead. The consciousness of loving and being loved brings a warmth and richness to life that nothing else can bring.

– Oscar Wilde (1854-1900), in conversation on the value of love.

The way to love anything is to realise that it may be lost.

– Gilbert K. Chesterton (1874-1936), *Tremendous Trifles* (1909) – often referred to as the 'prince of paradox.'

Poetry makes nothing happen.

– W.H. Auden

The Writers On... Series hopes to show that words, crafted well, with thought, precision and imagination, can have a lasting impact on the world around us.

A good quotation can illuminate meaning, provide evidence or inspiration, pay homage or merely make the user seem well-read.

But what is the importance of being 'well-read'? Literature, although pleasing and entertaining in itself, is so much more than that. Like all the creative arts, it preserves ideals, and is often the last thing left to speak across the ages. It makes the otherwise non-existent, un-envisaged, and un-spoken widely available. As W.H. Auden so aptly states, 'Poetry makes nothing happen.' And this nothingness is exactly the point. With the act of reading, good writing makes the previously un-imagined, *possible*. Through poetry and prose, nothing becomes something.

Dealing with any aspect of our daily lives, from serious topics such as love and the environment, to sensual pleasures such as food, drink or sex – it is good to bear in mind those words which have peaked our awareness. With this collection of some of the greatest, *Writers On…* the reader will hopefully never be short of possibilities.

Also in the *Writers On...* Series

Writers On... NATURE
Amelia Carruthers

Writers On... ATHEISM
Amelia Carruthers

Writers On... FOOD
Amelia Carruthers

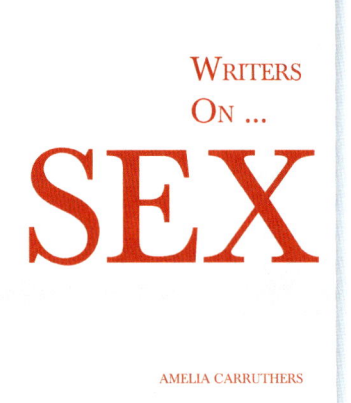

Writers On... SEX
Amelia Carruthers

Printed in Great Britain
by Amazon